EMMA FARRARONS is a French illustrator and graphic designer. Born on the island of Cebu in the Philippines, Emma grew up in Paris.

She was trained in illustration at the Edinburgh College of Art and l'École nationale supérieure des Arts Décoratifs. After completing a textile and printmaking course at Capellagården school in Sweden, she developed a particular love for pattern and fabric print and is inspired by French, Scandinavian, and Japanese design. She illustrates and designs books, posters, and stationery.

When she is not drawing and designing, Emma enjoys cooking, sewing, travel, and practicing mindfulness. She lives in London with her Danish husband.

ALSO BY EMMA FARRARONS

A to Z of Style by Amy de la Haye,
illustrated by Emma Farrarons

THE
MINDFULNESS
COLORING BOOK

THE EXPERIMENT

BECAUSE EVERY BOOK IS A TEST OF NEW IDEAS

THE
MINDFULNESS
COLORING BOOK

Anti-Stress Art Therapy for Busy People

Emma Farrarons

THE EXPERIMENT
NEW YORK

The Mindfulness Coloring Book: *Anti-Stress Art Therapy for Busy People*

Copyright © 2015 Emma Farrarons

First published in Great Britain in 2015 by Boxtree, an imprint of Pan Macmillan, a division of Macmillan Publishers Limited.

The Experiment, LLC
220 East 23rd Street, Suite 301
New York, NY 10010-4674
www.theexperimentpublishing.com

The Experiment's books are available at special discounts when purchased in bulk for premiums and sales promotions as well as for fund-raising or educational use. For details, contact us at info@theexperimentpublishing.com.

Library of Congress Cataloging-in-Publication Data

Farrarons, Emma.
  The mindfulness coloring book : anti-stress art therapy for busy people / Emma Farrarons.
     pages cm
  ISBN 978-1-61519-282-3 (pbk.) 1. Coloring books. 2. Stress management--Miscellanea. I. Title.
  NC965.9.F37 2015
  741.023--dc23
                              2015006023

ISBN 978-1-61519-282-3

Cover design by Sarah Schneider
Cover illustrations by Emma Farrarons

Manufactured in the United States of America
Distributed by Workman Publishing Company, Inc.
Distributed simultaneously in Canada by Thomas Allen & Son Ltd.

First printing June 2015
10 9 8

For Asger Bruun Jakobsen

INTRODUCTION

We all lead busy lives, rushing around on autopilot, dashing from place to place, multi-tasking at work, taking care of our families and trying to stay in touch with friends. But we now know that taking a moment to pause and be mindful can dramatically improve our well-being, making us feel calmer, less stressed, and more at peace with our emotions.

Being mindful is about paying attention to the present moment, clearing your mind of distractions, and focusing on simply being. Pretty much any activity, done right, can be an exercise in mindfulness—walking down the street, eating a piece of chocolate, or simply breathing in and out. But the act of coloring—carefully and attentively filling a page with color, the feel of the pencil in your hand as you meditate on the beauty of the whole illustration— is particularly suited to mindful meditation.

The exquisite scenes and intricate sophisticated patterns in this little coloring book offer a perfect calming exercise in mindfulness and creativity. Whatever you are doing, wherever you are, we hope you will enjoy these beautiful drawings. Color in, de-stress, and be mindful.

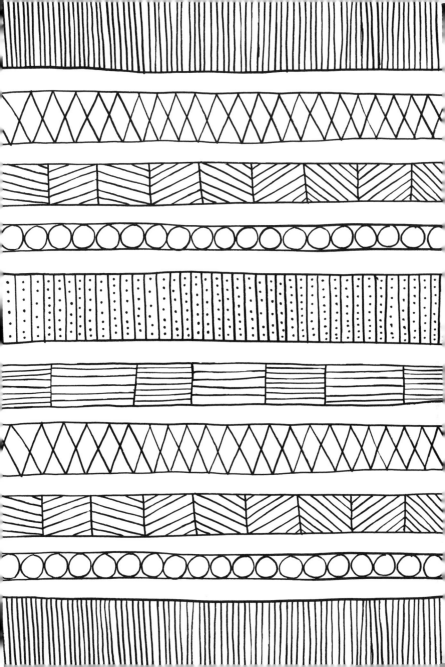

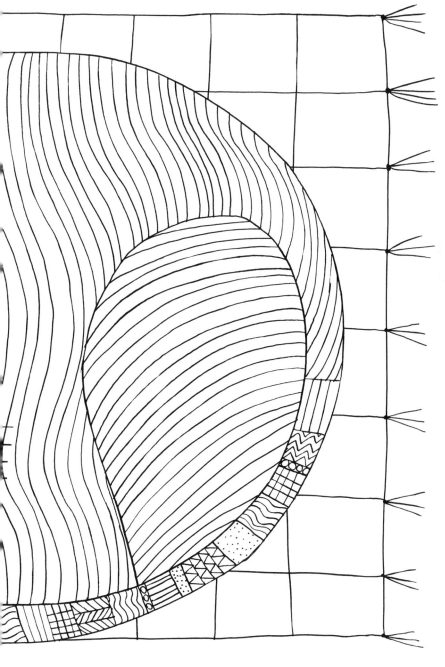

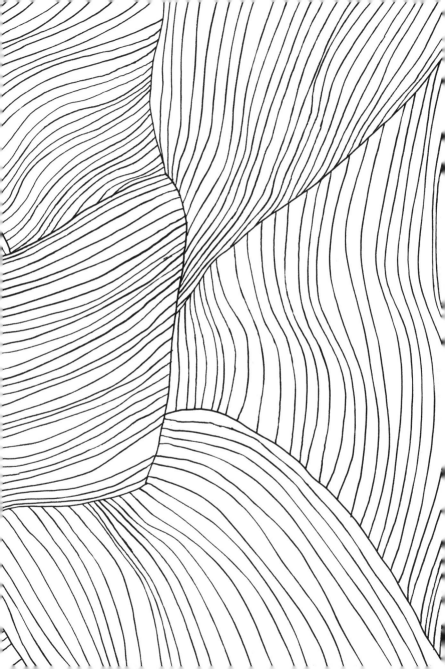

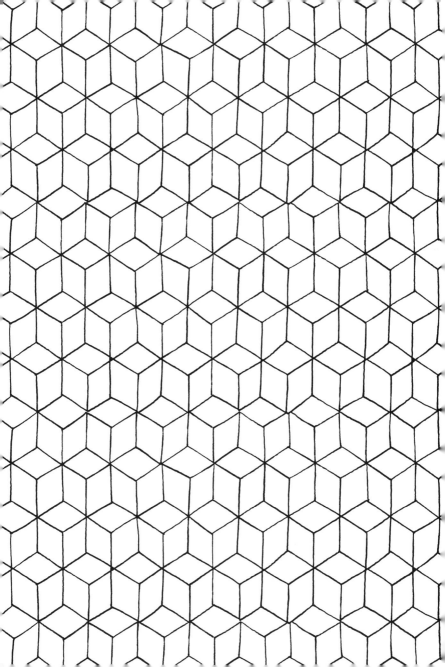

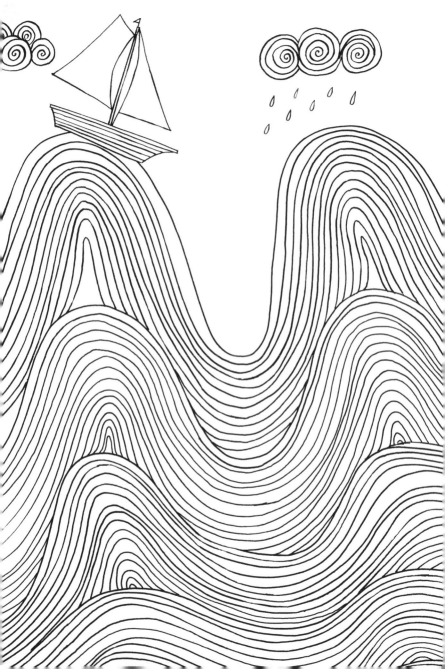

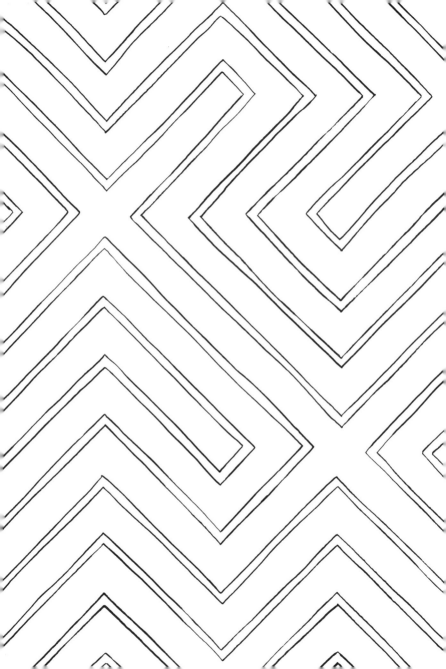

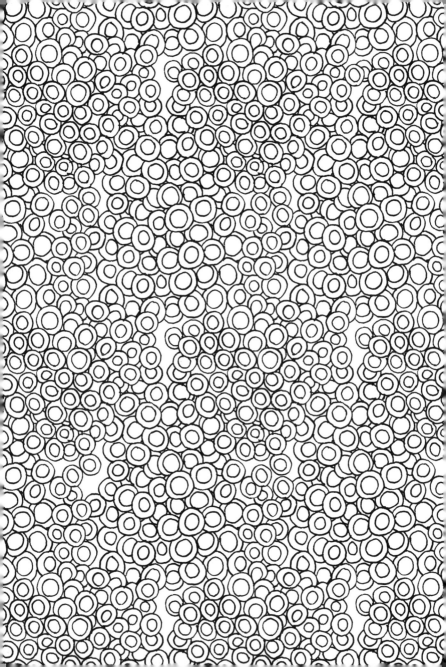

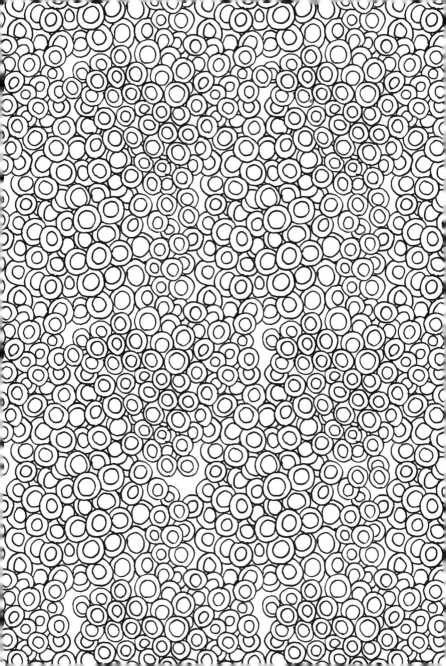

THANKS

I would like to thank my parents for taking me to a painting atelier every Wednesday afternoon. A special thank you to Cindy Chan—my cabbage pattern is dedicated to you.

EMMA FARRARONS

illustration & art direction

www.emmafarrarons.com